First Grade
CD-ROM and Workbook

Written by
Lorie DeYoung
Mary Vivian
Elizabeth Strauss

Illustrated by
Robin Michal Koontz
Laura Rader

©1997 School Zone Publishing Company

RESOURCE GUIDE

Your child will enter a world of learning play with the *First Grade* CD-ROM and workbook.

FIRST GRADE CD-ROM

- Improve memory skills by matching pictures to pictures or pictures to words.

- Sequence letters or numbers in dot-to-dot pictures. Each completed scene has a surprise color and sound reward.

- Read along with a delightful story about colors. Watch entertaining movies to learn about basic shapes.

- Draw, paint, and color delightful scenes. Pictures can be printed in black and white or color.

- Listen and laugh at silly knock, knock jokes.

- Click on the ring in the upper left corner for helpful hints.

Main Menu

Children will return again and again to enjoy the activities on the *First Grade* CD-ROM. Matching pictures, recognizing words, listening to a story, completing dot-to-dot pictures, drawing, and painting all add up to learning fun.

FIRST GRADE Workbook

Included with the CD-ROM is a workbook that reviews important first grade skills. Addition, subtraction, consonant and vowel review, and beginning reading are just some of the concepts covered in the following pages.

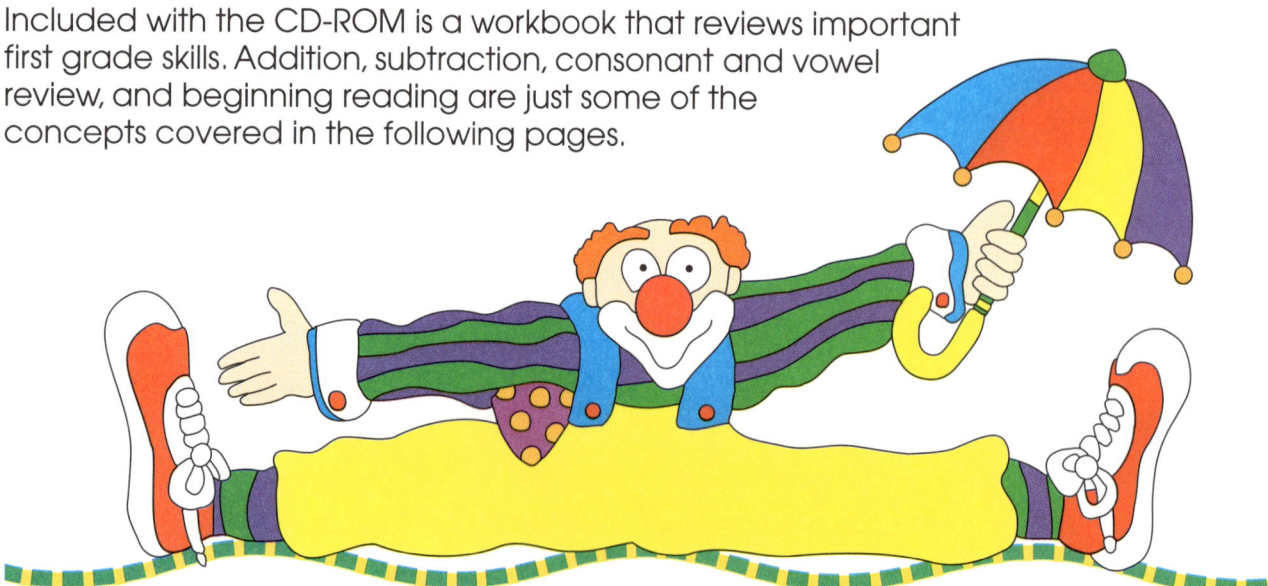

©1997 School Zone Publishing Company

More Learning Fun

1. **Create Story Problems** As you and your child go about your daily routine, create addition and subtraction story problems. For example, when you set the table, tell how many plates you are holding. Then change the number each time you set a plate down on the table. When you take a trip to the playground, invent story problems based on children arriving at and leaving the swing set, the climbing structure, or the sandbox. Encourage your child to make up story problems, too.

2. **Collect Words** Give your child a box that will hold 3" x 5" cards. Each day have your child choose a word to learn. Write the word on a 3" x 5" card and give it to your child. Your child may want to decorate the word card with markers or crayons before storing it in the word box. Encourage your child to take the cards out of the box and read them. Help your child with any word that he or she has forgotten. Children need lots of practice to recognize words.

3. **Make Silly Sentences** Purchase a set of sentence-making cards, or create a set on 3" x 5" cards. One-third of the cards should contain adjectives, or describing words, such as *silly, funny, large,* and *tired*. One-third should contain plural nouns, or naming words, such as *dogs, girls,* and *boats*. One-third should contain verbs, or action words, such as *bark, giggle,* and *run*. To make forming sentences easier, use a different color pen for each type of card. Review the words on the cards to make sure your child can read them. Ask your child to select an adjective card, a noun card, and a verb card and place them in a row to make a sentence. Read the silly sentence. Then mix up the cards and create another sentence. As your child learns new words, add them to the card sets.

4. **Make a Book** Staple sheets of blank paper together. Ask your child to make up a story. Have your child tell who the story is about and what will happen to that character. Decide whether you or your child will write the words of the story in the book. Encourage your child to illustrate the story. Read the story to your child and have your child read the story to you.

©1997 School Zone Publishing Company

Addition Facts 1-6

The answer to an addition problem is called the **sum**.
You write the problem like this: **2 + 3 = 5**. 5 is the sum.

$\underline{\ 2\ } + \underline{\ 3\ } = \underline{\ 5\ }$

Write the addition problems and the sums.

1.    ____ + ____ = ____

2.    ____ + ____ = ____

3.    ____ + ____ = ____

4.    ____ + ____ = ____

5.    ____ + ____ = ____

6.    ____ + ____ = ____

7. 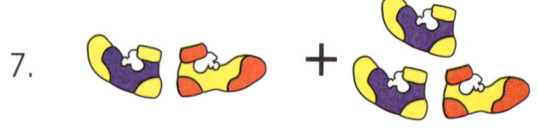   ____ + ____ = ____

More Addition Facts 1-6

Try using this number line to find the sum of 4 + 2.
Start at 4. Count forward 2 numbers. That's your answer!

The sum of 4 + 2 is 6.

Find each sum. Use the number line for help.

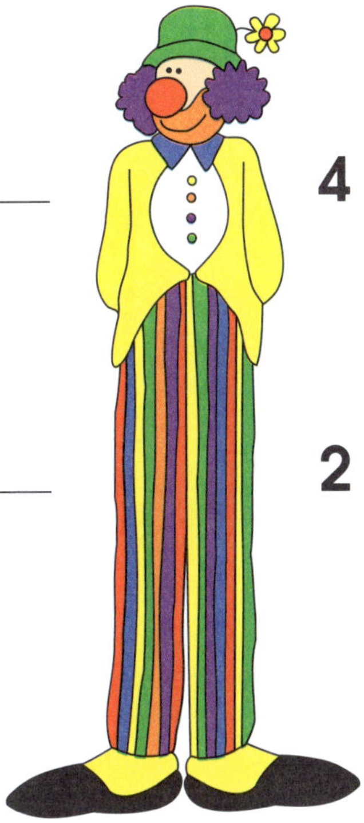

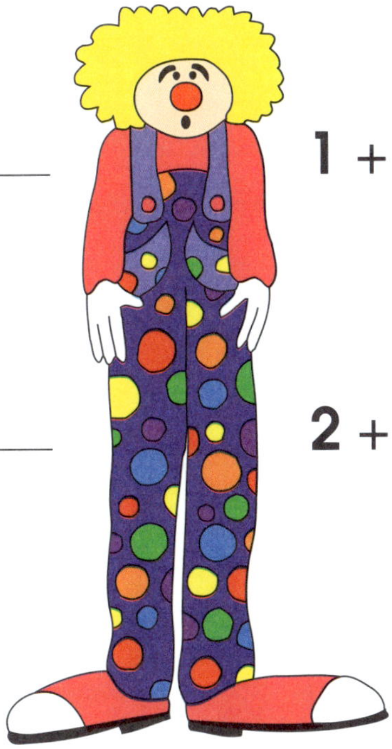

1. 3 + 3 = ____   1 + 4 = ____   4 + 2 = ____

2. 5 + 1 = ____   2 + 3 = ____   2 + 2 = ____

3. 4   2   3   1   5
   +1   +4   +3   +1   +0

4. 2   1   4   3   1
   +2   +2   +0   +2   +3

Subtraction Facts 1-6

The answer to a subtraction problem is called the **difference**.
The difference for this picture is 2.

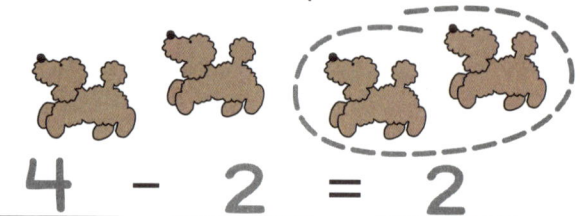

Write the subtraction problems and the differences.

 1.  ___ - ___ = ___

 2.  ___ - ___ = ___

3.  ___ - ___ = ___

4.  ___ - ___ = ___

5.  ___ - ___ = ___

6.  ___ - ___ = ___

7.  ___ - ___ = ___

©1997 School Zone Publishing Company

More Subtraction Facts 1-6

Try using this number line to find the difference of 6 – 4. Start at 6. Count back 4 numbers. That's your answer!

The difference of 6 – 4 is 2.

Find the differences. Use the number line for help.

1. 6 – 3 = _____   5 – 2 = _____   4 – 2 = _____

2. 3 – 2 = _____   3 – 1 = _____   2 – 1 = _____

3. 5   6
   -1   -4
   ___   ___

4. 5   4   6   6
   -0   -2   -3   -5
   ___   ___   ___   ___

5. 5   4   3   4
   -2   -3   -2   -0
   ___   ___   ___   ___

©1997 School Zone Publishing Company

Family of Facts 1-6

A **family of facts** uses the same numbers.
Meet the family of 5.

$3 + 2 = 5$
$2 + 3 = 5$
$5 - 2 = 3$
$5 - 3 = 2$

Find the answers for each **fact family**.

1. 3   6
   +3   -3

2. 1   2
   +1   -1

3. 2   4
   +2   -2

4. 5   1   6   6
   +1   +5   -5   -1

5. 4   2   6   6
   +2   +4   -4   -2

6. 1   3   4   4
   +3   +1   -1   -3

8   ©1997 School Zone Publishing Company

Adding and Subtracting 0 and 1

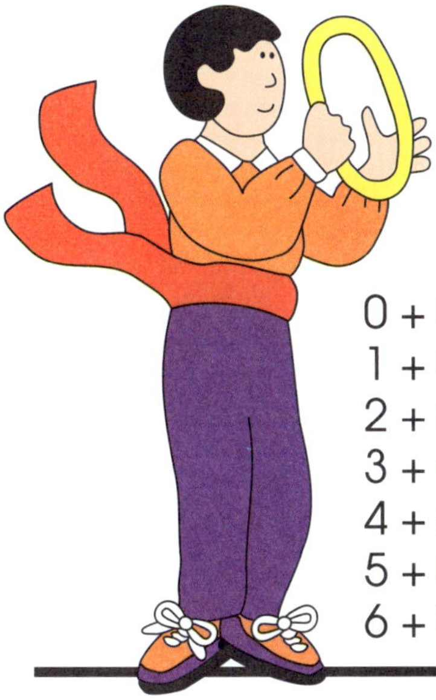

```
0 + 0 = 0              0 - 0 = 0
1 + 0 = 1              1 - 0 = 1     1 - 1 = 0
2 + 0 = 2   1 + 1 = 2  2 - 0 = 2     2 - 1 = 1
3 + 0 = 3   2 + 1 = 3  3 - 0 = 3     3 - 1 = 2
4 + 0 = 4   3 + 1 = 4  4 - 0 = 4     4 - 1 = 3
5 + 0 = 5   4 + 1 = 5  5 - 0 = 5     5 - 1 = 4
6 + 0 = 6   5 + 1 = 6  6 - 0 = 6     6 - 1 = 5
```

Find the sums.

1.
   4   2   5   1   2
　+0　　+1　　+1　　+4　　+0

2.
   4   3   2   1   3
　+2　　+3　　+3　　+3　　+2

Find the differences.

3.
   3   2   4   3   1
　−1　　−1　　−1　　−0　　−1

4.
   5   5   0   4   3
　−3　　−4　　−0　　−4　　−2

More Adding and Subtracting

Write the sums and differences.
The first one is done for you.

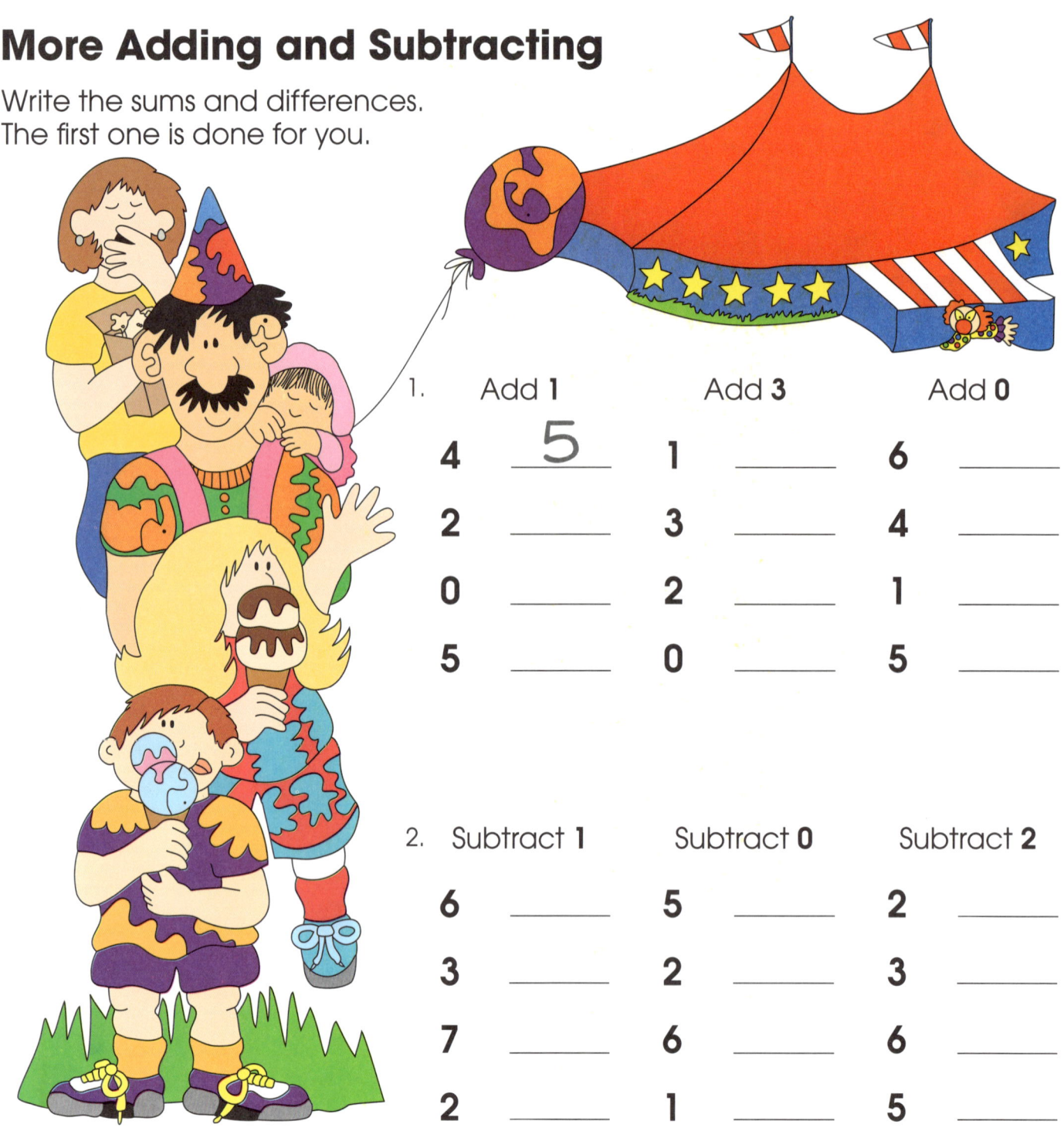

1. Add **1**   Add **3**   Add **0**

    4 ___5___   1 _____   6 _____

    2 _____   3 _____   4 _____

    0 _____   2 _____   1 _____

    5 _____   0 _____   5 _____

2. Subtract **1**   Subtract **0**   Subtract **2**

    6 _____   5 _____   2 _____

    3 _____   2 _____   3 _____

    7 _____   6 _____   6 _____

    2 _____   1 _____   5 _____

How many hidden elephants are in the picture?
Finish the table to find the answer.

2	+ 4	− 3	− 1	+ 2	=	

elephants

Addition Facts 7 and 8

Pictures can help us learn facts!

Write the addition problems and the sums.

1.  ___ + ___ = ___
2.  ___ + ___ = ___
3.  ___ + ___ = ___
4. 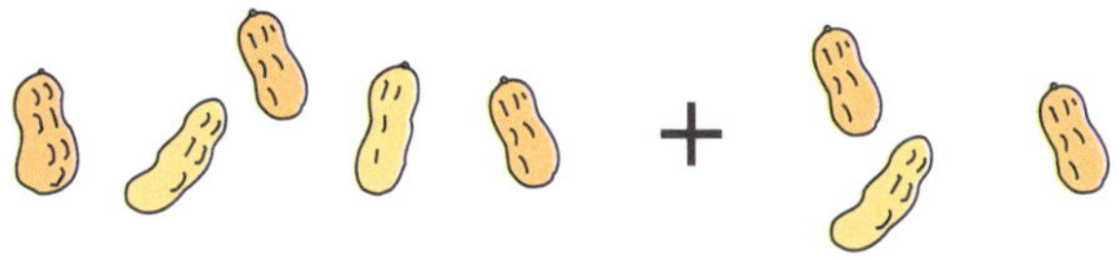 ___ + ___ = ___
5.  ___ + ___ = ___
6.  ___ + ___ = ___
7. 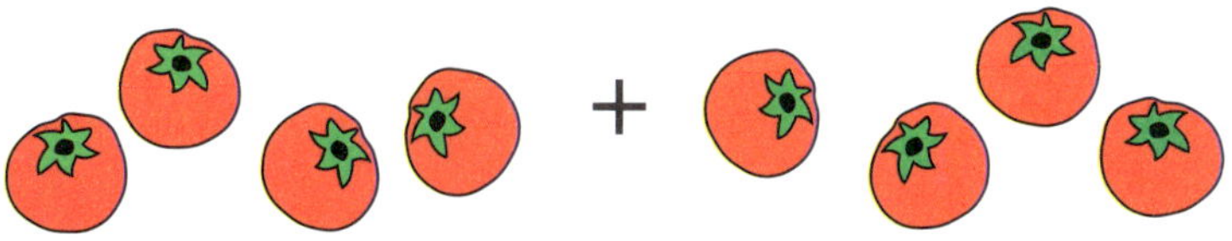 ___ + ___ = ___

Subtraction Facts 7 and 8

Write subtraction problems and the differences.
The first problem is done for you.

1. 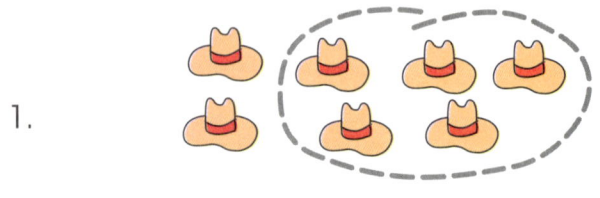   7 - 5 = 2

2.   ___ - ___ = ___

3.   ___ - ___ = ___

4.    ___ - ___ = ___

5.    ___ - ___ = ___

6.   ___ - ___ = ___

7.   ___ - ___ = ___

Practice Facts 7 and 8

Find the sum or difference for each problem.

1. 4 + 3 = ___   6 + 2 = ___   8 − 4 = ___

2. 8 − 3 = ___   1 + 6 = ___   7 − 4 = ___

3. 2 + 5 = ___   7 + 1 = ___   8 − 2 = ___

4. 6   7   0   8   8
   +2   −2   +7   −2   −5

5. 7   8   5   7   4
   −5   −3   +3   −3   +4

Family of Facts 7 and 8

$5 + 3 = 8$ $3 + 5 = 8$ $8 - 5 = 3$ $8 - 3 = 5$

Find the answers for each fact family.

1.   4   3   7   7   2.   7   7
      +3   +4   −4   −3   +0   −0

3.   4   8   4.   2   5   7   7
     +4   −4   +5   +2   −2   −5

5.   2   6   8   8
     +6   +2   −2   −6

6.   7   1   8   8
     +1   +7   −7   −1

7.   8   8
     +0   −0

Addition Facts 9 and 10

Write the addition problems and the sums.

1.  ____ + ____ = ____

2. 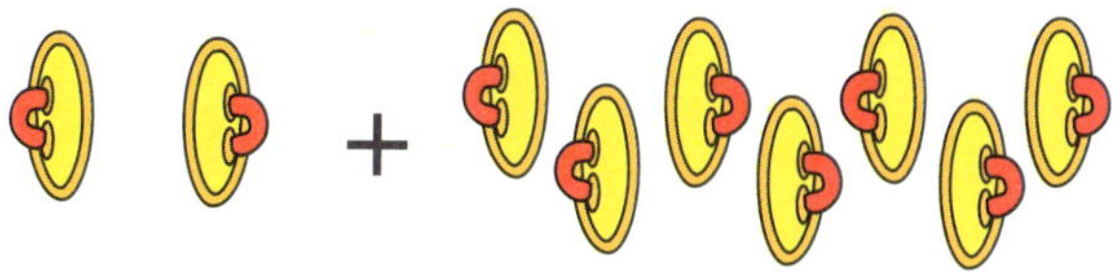 ____ + ____ = ____

3. 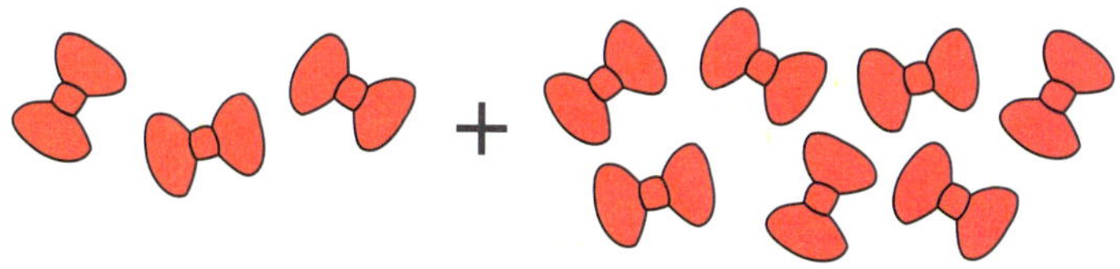 ____ + ____ = ____

4. 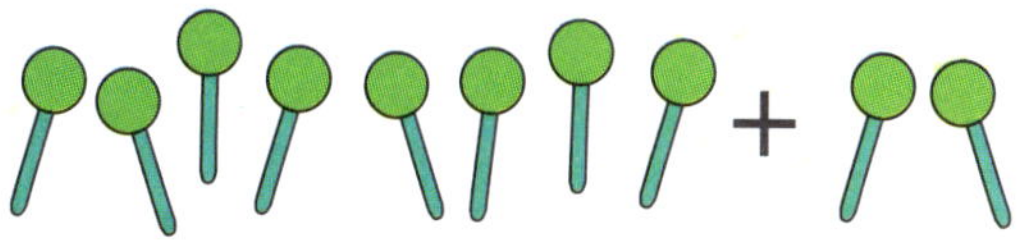 ____ + ____ = ____

5. 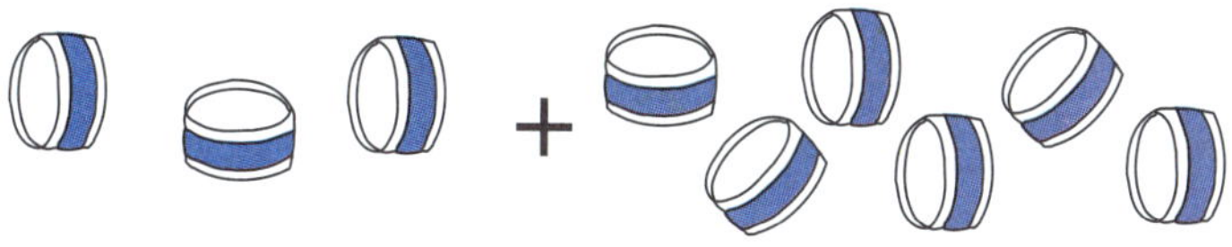 ____ + ____ = ____

6. 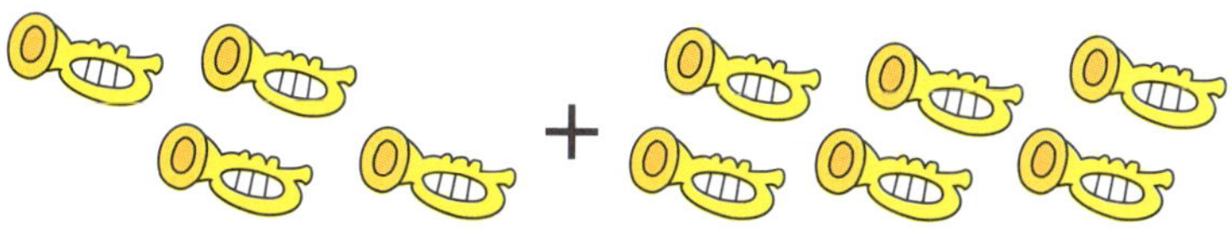 ____ + ____ = ____

7. 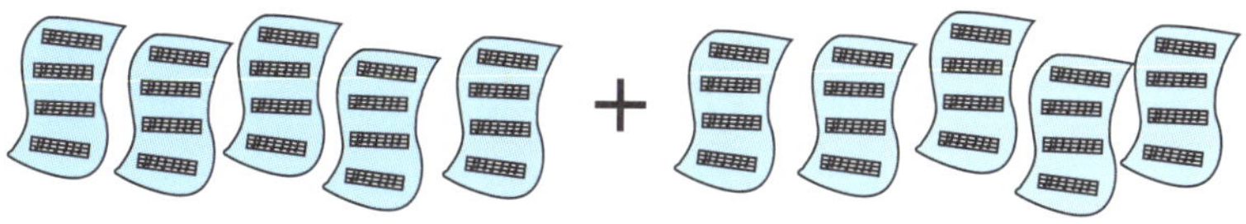 ____ + ____ = ____

Subtraction Facts 9 and 10

Write the subtraction problems and the differences.

1. _____ − _____ = _____

2. _____ − _____ = _____

3. _____ − _____ = _____

4. _____ − _____ = _____

5. _____ − _____ = _____

6. _____ − _____ = _____

7. _____ − _____ = _____

Family of Facts 9 and 10

8 + 1 = 9
1 + 8 = 9
9 − 8 = 1
9 − 1 = 8

Find the answers for each fact family.

1. 6   3   9   9
   +3   +6   −6   −3

2. 5   4   9   9
   +4   +5   −5   −4

3. 6   4   10   10
   +4   +6   −6   −4

4. 7   3   10   10
   +3   +7   −7   −3

5. 2   8   10   10
   +8   +2   −2   −8

©1997 School Zone Publishing Company   17

Practice Facts 9 and 10

Find the sum or difference for each problem.

1. 9 − 3 = ____   4 + 5 = ____   9 − 4 = ____

2. 5 + 5 = ____   9 − 7 = ____   10 − 2 = ____

3. 4 + 6 = ____   10 − 4 = ____   7 + 2 = ____

4. 7   8   9
   +3   +2   −0

5. 9   9   3
   −6   −2   +7

6. 6   10   9
   +4   −5   −1

Practice Addition and Subtraction 1 – 10

Find the sum or difference for each problem.

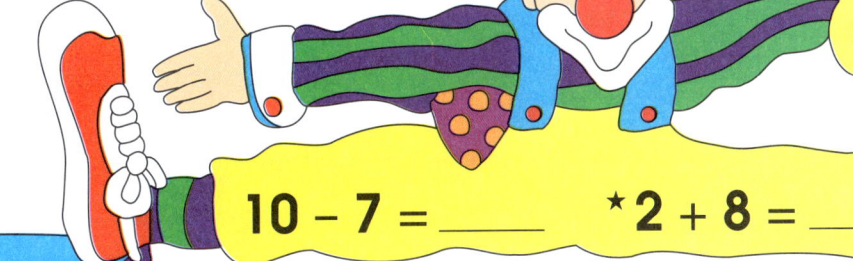

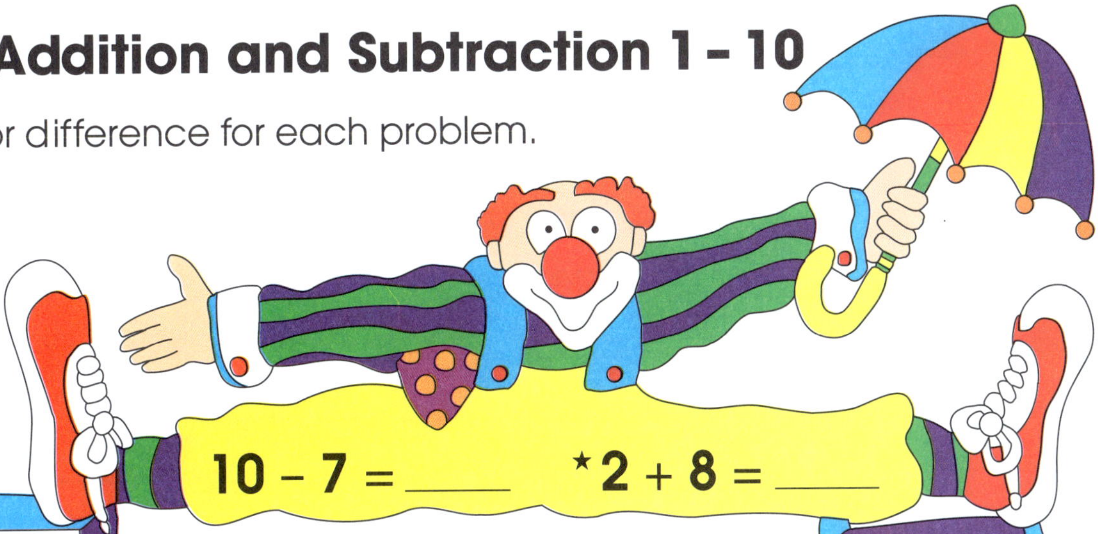

10 − 7 = ____   ★2 + 8 = ____

Ladder 1

$$\begin{array}{r}0\\+4\\\hline\end{array}$$

$$\begin{array}{r}9\\-2\\\hline\end{array}$$

$$\begin{array}{r}10\\-8\\\hline\end{array}$$

$$\begin{array}{r}9\\-3\\\hline\end{array}$$

$$\begin{array}{r}3\\+4\\\hline\end{array}$$

$$\begin{array}{r}6\\+3\\\hline\end{array}$$

Ladder 2

$$\begin{array}{r}7\\+3\\\hline\end{array}$$

$$\begin{array}{r}10\\-0\\\hline\end{array}$$

$$\begin{array}{r}5\\+2\\\hline\end{array}$$

$$\begin{array}{r}9\\-6\\\hline\end{array}$$

$$\begin{array}{r}4\\+4\\\hline\end{array}$$

$$\begin{array}{r}7\\+2\\\hline\end{array}$$

5 + 4 = ____

3 + 5 = ____

6 + 4 = ____

8 − 5 = ____

10 − 2 = ____

It's beary easy!

Practice Facts 1 – 10

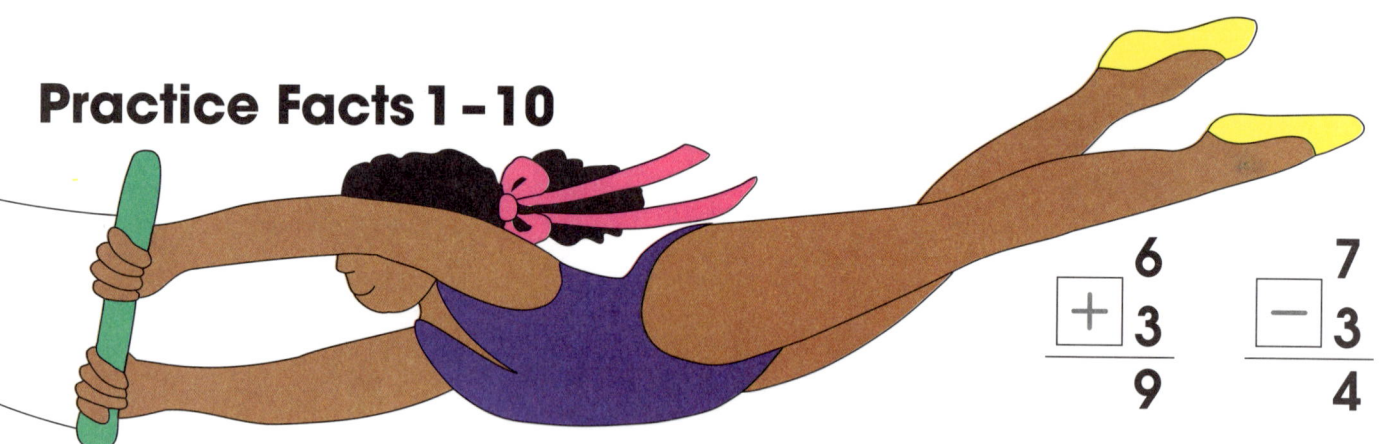

Fill in the blanks with + or – to make the sums or differences true.

1.
□ 5
  5
―――
10

□ 6
  2
―――
4

□ 5
  3
―――
2

□ 8
  2
―――
10

2.
□ 8
  5
―――
3

□ 2
  6
―――
8

□ 6
  4
―――
2

□ 7
  1
―――
6

3.
□ 6
  3
―――
9

□ 9
  4
―――
5

□ 8
  6
―――
2

□ 2
  5
―――
7

4.
□ 2
  6
―――
8

□ 9
  5
―――
4

□ 7
  4
―――
3

□ 4
  6
―――
10

It's not as hard as it looks!

Fact Families of 11

Work on these facts for the family of 11.
There are 12 lions. Use them as a number line, if you need help.

1.
```
  2      9     11     11
 +9     +2    - 2    - 9
```

2.
```
  4      7     11     11
 +7     +4    - 4    - 7
```

3.
```
 10      1     11     11
 + 1   +10    -10    - 1
```

4.
```
  5      6     11     11
 +6     +5    - 5    - 6
```

©1997 School Zone Publishing Company

Fact Families of 12

Work on these facts for the family of 12.

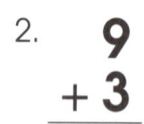

1.   4   8   12   12
    +8   +4   − 4   − 8

2.   9   3   12   12
    +3   +9   − 9   − 3

3.   11   1   12   12
    + 1   +11   −11   − 1

4.   5   7   12   12
    +7   +5   − 5   − 7

You charm the skin off me!

Practice Facts 1-12

Find the sum or difference.
Circle the clown with the greatest total.
He will jump into the bucket first.

Counting On to Add

Counting on helps you find the sum faster.
To count on, start with the **greatest** number (5). $5 + 3 = 8$
Count **3** numbers more **6, 7, 8**. The sum is **8**.

Find the sum for each problem. Count on if you need help.

1. **8 + 3** = _____   **2 + 7** = _____   **5 + 5** = _____

2. **6 + 6** = _____   **9 + 2** = _____   **7 + 4** = _____

3. **11 + 1** = _____   **4 + 8** = _____   **3 + 5** = _____

4.   9   4   7
   +3   +4   +5
   ---   ---   ---

5.   5   8   6
   +6   +2   +3
   ---   ---   ---

6.   4   5   6
   +3   +4   +4
   ---   ---   ---

Counting Back to Subtract

Counting back helps you find the difference faster.
To count back, start with the greatest number (**11**). **11 – 5 = 6**
Count **5** numbers back **10, 9, 8, 7, 6**. The difference is **6**.

Find the difference for each problem. Count back if you need help.

1. 12 – 7 = _____   11 – 7 = _____   10 – 8 = _____

2. 11 – 2 = _____   10 – 2 = _____   10 – 6 = _____

3. 12 – 5 = _____   11 – 5 = _____

4.   12   11   10
   – 8   – 7   – 5

5.   12   9   11
   – 3   – 4   – 6

6.   12   12   12
   – 6   – 4   – 8

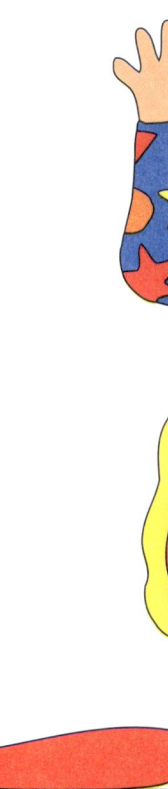

©1997 School Zone Publishing Company

Practice Counting On and Counting Back

Find the sums and the differences to solve the riddle.
Use the code to find the answer.

Sometimes people call them kings.
At the circus, they jump through rings.

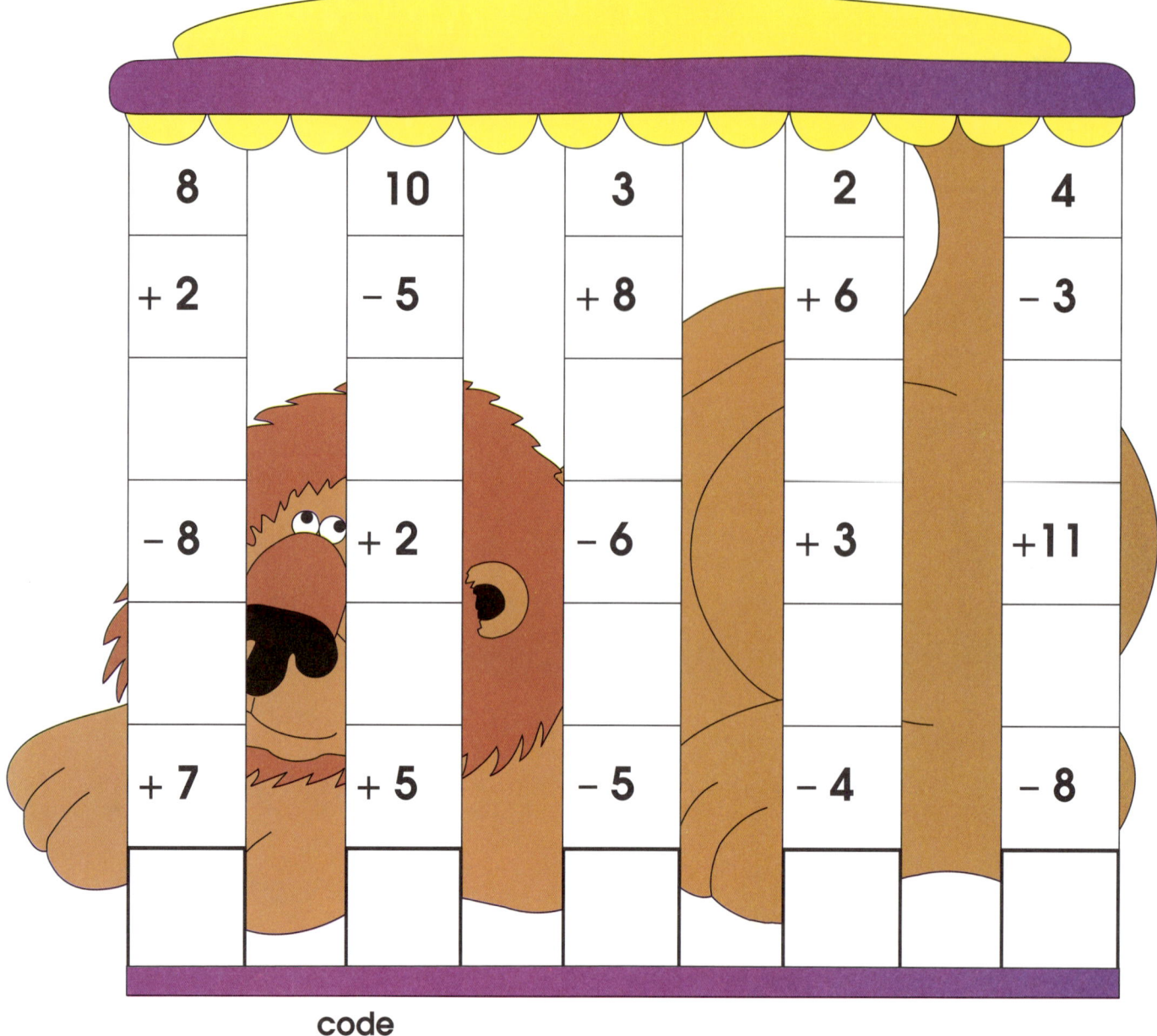

8	10	3	2	4
+ 2	− 5	+ 8	+ 6	− 3
− 8	+ 2	− 6	+ 3	+11
+ 7	+ 5	− 5	− 4	− 8

code

0 1 2 3 4 5 6 7 8 9 10 11 12
o z e b s r k n h l f p i

____ ____ ____ ____ ____

Adding Three Addends

To add three numerals (addends) together you
1. Add the 5 + 4.
2. Then add the sum of 9 to the 2. The sum is 11.

$$\begin{array}{r}5\\4\\+2\\\hline 11\end{array} = 9$$

Find the sums.

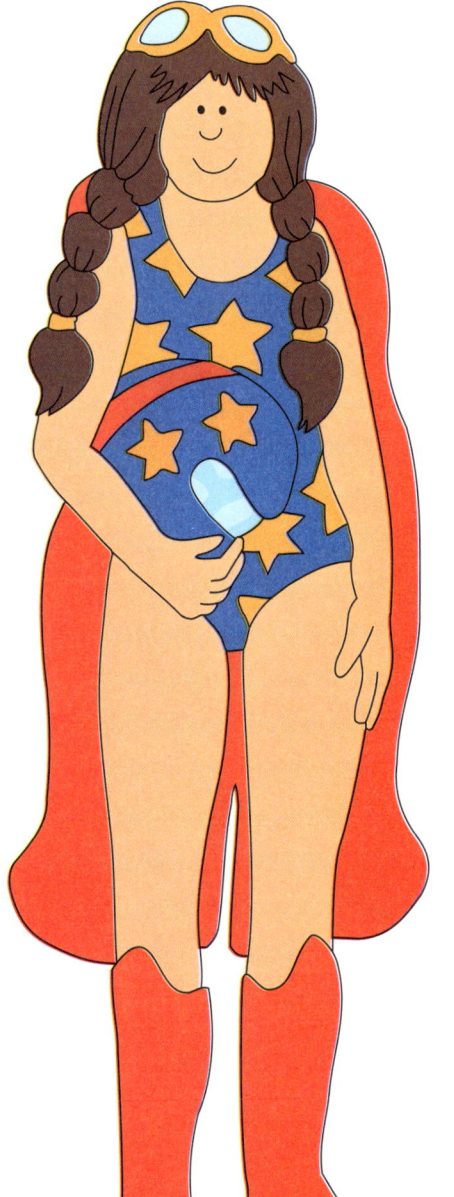

1.   2   1   9   2
      6   8   1   4
    +3   +3   +2   +5

2.   4   4   3   5
      7   4   1   5
    +1   +2   +7   +2

3.   6   4   3   1
      2   4   2   2
    +2   +4   +5   +8

Adding Tens and Ones

1. Add the ones. 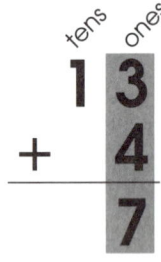 2. Then add the tens.

Add the ones. Then add the tens.

1.
   tens ones
   63   91   50
+ 5   + 6   + 8

2.
   72   25   53
+ 1   + 3   + 6

3.
   45   27   44
+ 14   + 60   + 34

28

Add More Tens and Ones

Add the ones and then the tens!

1. 56   71   43   20
   +20   +15   +32   +48

2. 81   90   85   34
   +10   + 7   +13   +35

3. 20   17   55   62
   +64   +12   +13   + 6

4. 47   21   40   26
   +30   + 6   +20   +53

Subtracting Tens and Ones

1. Subtract the ones.      2. Then subtract the tens.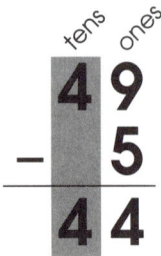

Subtract the ones.   Then subtract the tens.

1. 57   25   89
   − 5   − 2   − 7

2. 38   24   98
   − 5   − 1   − 6

3. 47   66   89
   −15   −23   −26

30
©1997 School Zone Publishing Company

Subtract More Tens and Ones

Subtract the ones and then the tens!

1.   58   77   45   26
     − 36   − 30   − 24   − 5

2.   86   38   67   53
     − 3   − 17   − 21   − 30

3.   99   85   78   37
     − 65   − 45   − 4   − 30

4.   48   59   76   87
     − 25   − 30   − 24   − 3

Adding and Subtracting Tens and Ones

Find each sum or difference.
Connect the dots from the least to the greatest number.

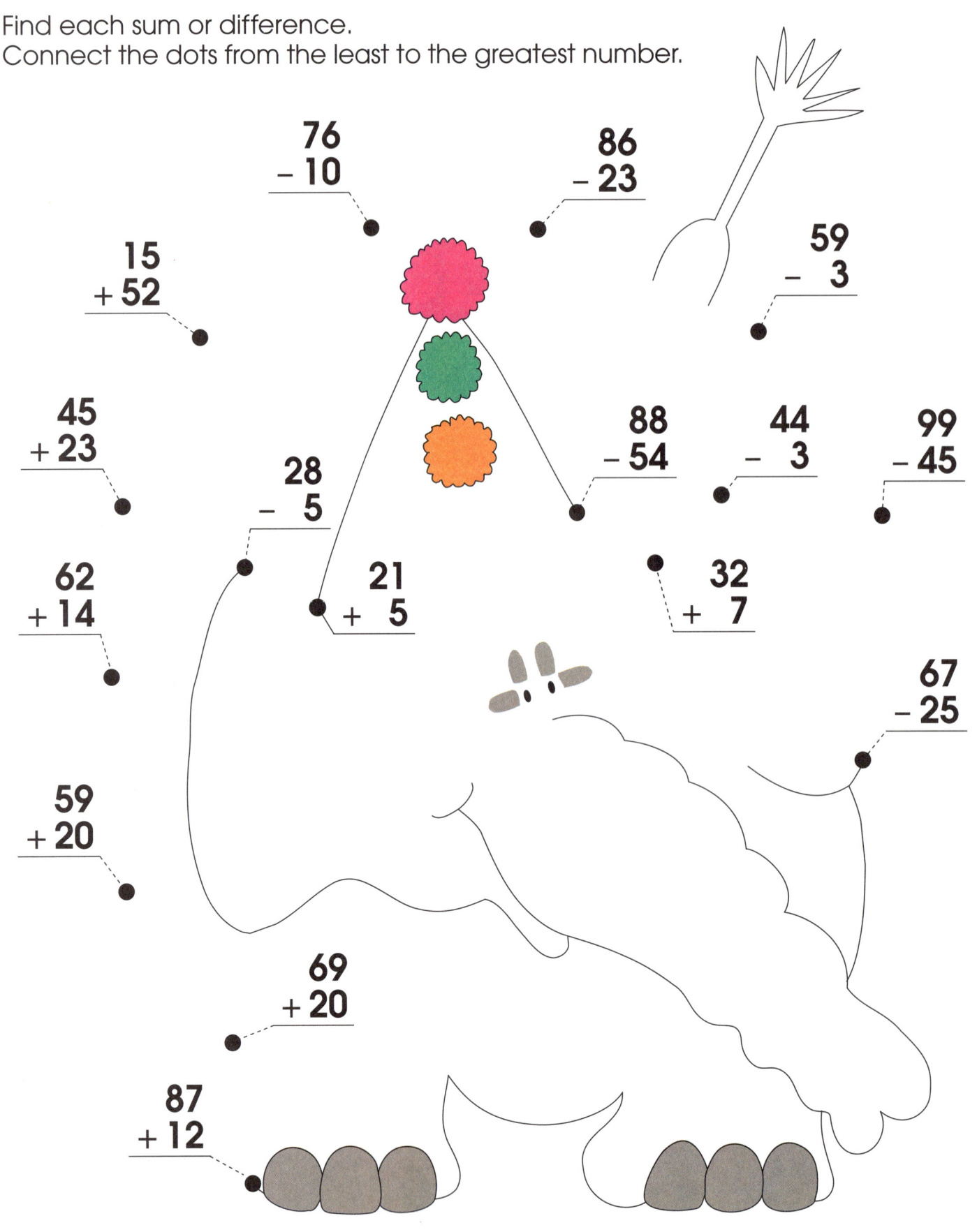

Grrrrrrrrr!

Finish the problems to help the lion tamer out of the cage.

Answer Key

Page 4
1. 2 + 2 = 4
2. 3 + 3 = 6
3. 4 + 2 = 6
4. 1 + 3 = 4
5. 1 + 1 = 2
6. 5 + 1 = 6
7. 2 + 3 = 5

Page 5
1. 6, 5, 6
2. 6, 5, 4
3. 5, 6, 6, 2, 5
4. 4, 3, 4, 5, 4

Page 6
1. 4 − 3 = 1
2. 6 − 3 = 3
3. 2 − 1 = 1
4. 5 − 2 = 3
5. 4 − 2 = 2
6. 6 − 4 = 2
7. 6 − 1 = 5

Page 7
1. 3, 3, 2
2. 1, 2, 1
3. 4, 2
4. 5, 2, 3, 1
5. 3, 1, 1, 4

Page 8
1. 6, 3
2. 2, 1
3. 4, 2
4. 6, 6, 1, 5
5. 6, 6, 2, 4
6. 4, 4, 3, 1

Page 9
1. 4, 3, 6, 5, 2
2. 6, 6, 5, 4, 5
3. 2, 1, 3, 3, 0
4. 2, 1, 0, 0, 1

Page 10
1.
Add 1	Add 3	Add 0
3	4	6
1	6	4
6	5	1
	3	5

2.
Subtract 1	Subtract 0	Subtract 2
5	5	0
2	2	1
6	6	4
1	1	3

| 2 | +4 | **6** | −3 | **3** | −1 | **2** | +2 | = | **4** |

Page 11
1. 3 + 4 = 7
2. 5 + 2 = 7
3. 1 + 6 = 7
4. 5 + 3 = 8
5. 7 + 1 = 8
6. 2 + 6 = 8
7. 4 + 4 = 8

Page 12
2. 7 − 4 = 3
3. 7 − 1 = 6
4. 7 − 3 = 4
5. 8 − 5 = 3
6. 7 − 0 = 7
7. 8 − 7 = 1

Page 13
1. 7, 8, 4
2. 5, 7, 3
3. 7, 8, 6
4. 8, 5, 7, 6, 3
5. 2, 5, 8, 4, 8

Page 14
1. 7, 7, 3, 4
2. 7, 7
3. 8, 4
4. 7, 7, 5, 2
5. 8, 8, 6, 2
6. 8, 8, 1, 7
7. 8, 8

Page 15
1. 4 + 5 = 9
2. 2 + 7 = 9
3. 3 + 7 = 10
4. 8 + 2 = 10
5. 3 + 6 = 9
6. 4 + 6 = 10
7. 5 + 5 = 10

Page 16
1. 9 − 4 = 5
2. 9 − 2 = 7
3. 9 − 6 = 3
4. 10 − 8 = 2
5. 10 − 4 = 6
6. 10 − 7 = 3
7. 10 − 5 = 5

Page 17
1. 9, 9, 3, 6
2. 9, 9, 4, 5
3. 10, 10, 4, 6
4. 10, 10, 3, 7
5. 10, 10, 8, 2

Page 18
1. 6, 9, 5
2. 10, 2, 8
3. 10, 6, 9
4. 10, 10, 9
5. 3, 7, 10
6. 10, 5, 8

©1997 School Zone Publishing Company

Answer Key

Page 19

Ladder 1	Center clockwise from star	Ladder 2
4	10	10
7	8	7
2	3	3
6	8	8
7	10	9
9	9	
	3	

Page 20
1. +, −, −, +
2. −, +, −, −
3. +, −, −, +
4. +, −, −, +

Page 21
1. 11, 11, 9, 2
2. 11, 11, 7, 4
3. 11, 11, 1, 10
4. 11, 11, 6, 5

Page 22
1. 12, 12, 8, 4
2. 12, 12, 3, 9
3. 12, 12, 1, 11
4. 12, 12, 7, 5

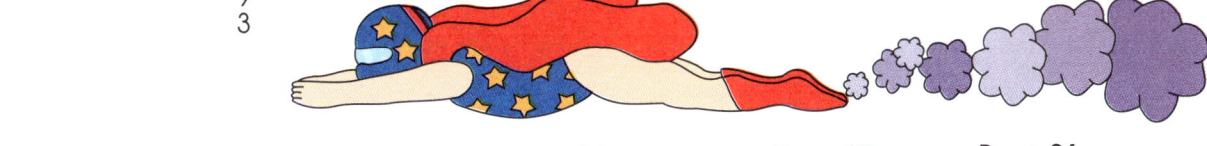

Page 23

10	4	12	0	7	5
+2	+7	−8	+9	−3	+2
12	11	4	9	4	7
−6	−6	−4	+2	+8	−4
6	5	0	11	12	3
−3	+5	+5	−7	−4	−2
3	10	5	4	8	1

Second clown from left should be circled.

Page 24
1. 11, 9, 10
2. 12, 11, 11
3. 12, 12, 8
4. 12, 8, 12
5. 11, 10, 9
6. 7, 9, 10

Page 25
1. 5, 4, 2
2. 9, 8, 4
3. 7, 6
4. 4, 4, 5
5. 9, 5, 5
6. 6, 8, 4

Page 26

8	10	3	2	4
+2	−5	+8	+6	−3
10	5	11	8	1
−8	+2	−6	+3	+11
2	7	5	11	12
+7	+5	−5	−4	−8
9	12	0	7	4

Code: lions

Page 27
1. 11, 12, 12, 11
2. 12, 10, 11, 12
3. 10, 12, 10, 11

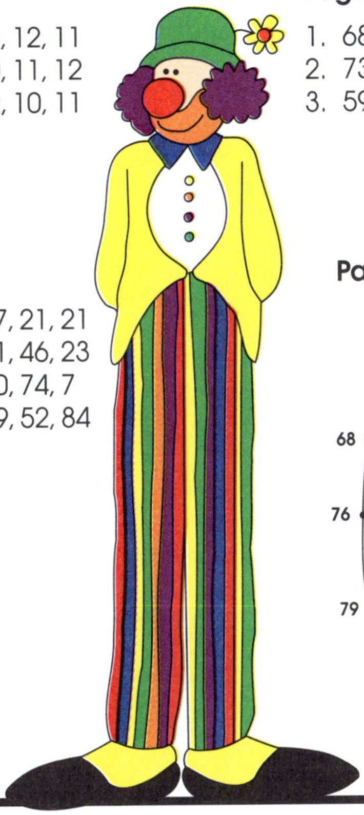

Page 28
1. 68, 97, 58
2. 73, 28, 59
3. 59, 87, 78

Page 29
1. 76, 86, 75, 68
2. 91, 97, 98, 69
3. 84, 29, 68, 68
4. 77, 27, 60, 79

Page 30
1. 52, 23, 82
2. 33, 23, 92
3. 32, 43, 63

Page 31
1. 22, 47, 21, 21
2. 83, 21, 46, 23
3. 34, 40, 74, 7
4. 23, 29, 52, 84

Page 32

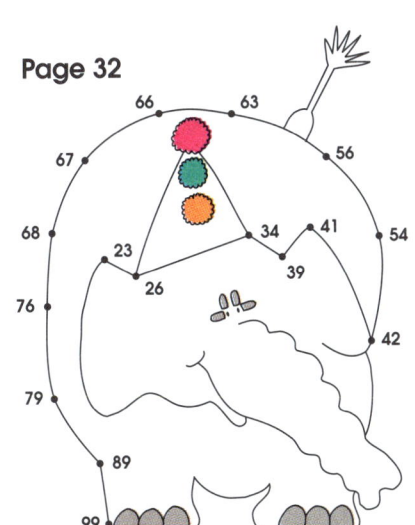

Page 33

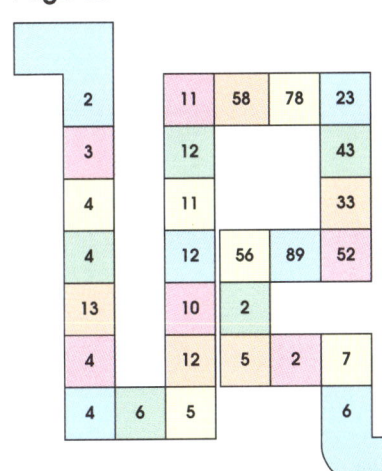

Beginning Sounds

Say the word for each picture.
Write the **beginning sound**.
Use these letters: **c, f, h, k, m, p, r, t.**

Beginning Sounds

Say the word for each picture.
Write the **beginning sound.**
Use these letters: **b, d, g, l, n, q, s, y.**

1. eaf
2. og
3. all
4. ueen
5. arn
6. oat
7. ine
8. oap

Ending Sounds

Say the word for each picture.
Write the **ending sound**.
Use these letters: **b, g, l, m, n, p, r, x.**

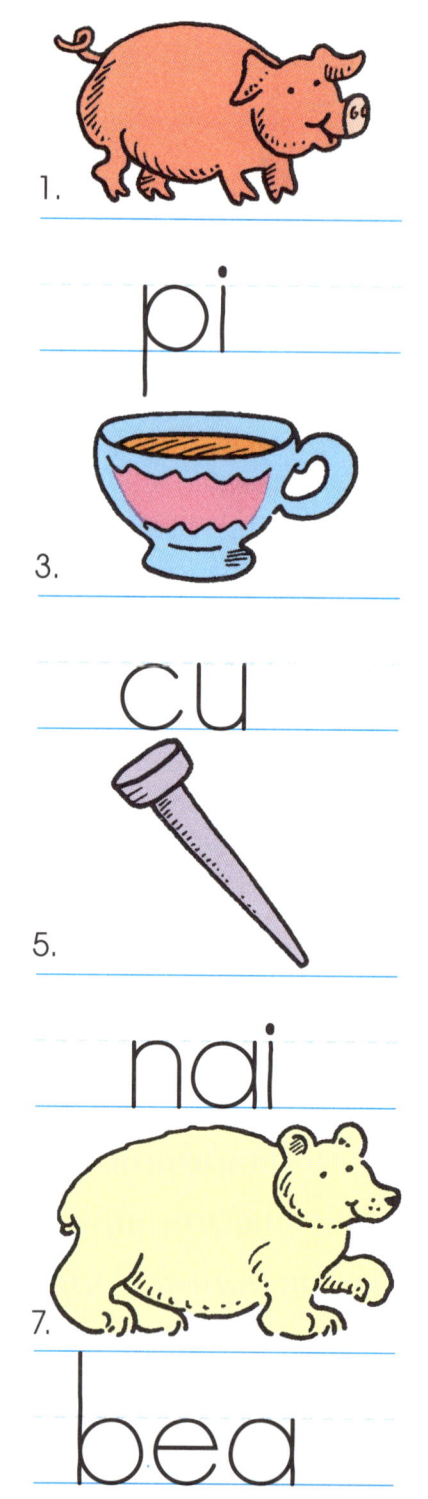

1.
2.

3. pi
4. su

5. cu
6. tu

7. nai
8. fo

bea
dru

Ending Sounds

Say the word for each picture.
Write the **ending sound**.
Use these letters: **d, f, k, l, o, s, t, r.**

1. be___
2. sea___
3. ca___
4. el___
5. ___zer
6. bu___
7. ca___
8. boo___

Review

Say the word for each picture.
Write the beginning and ending sounds.
Use these letters: **m, n, p, s, g, t, b**.

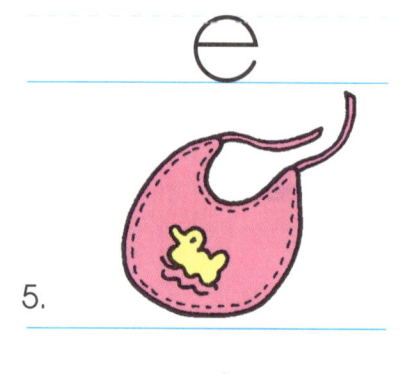

1. _ a _

2. _ o _

3. _ e _

4. _ u _

5. _ i _

6. _ a _

7. _ u _

8. _ e _

Words with Short a and Short e

Write a **short a** word from the box in each blank.

> nap   maps
> bat   Dad

Sam walks to school.

_____

He learns about _____.

_____

At recess he plays with a ball and _____.

_____ drives him home.

Sam is tired, so he takes a _____.

Circle the **short e** words.

| tent | bed | let | key |
| see | pen | she | net |

Words with Short i

Write the **short i** words.
Then color the **short i** words in the picture **pink**.

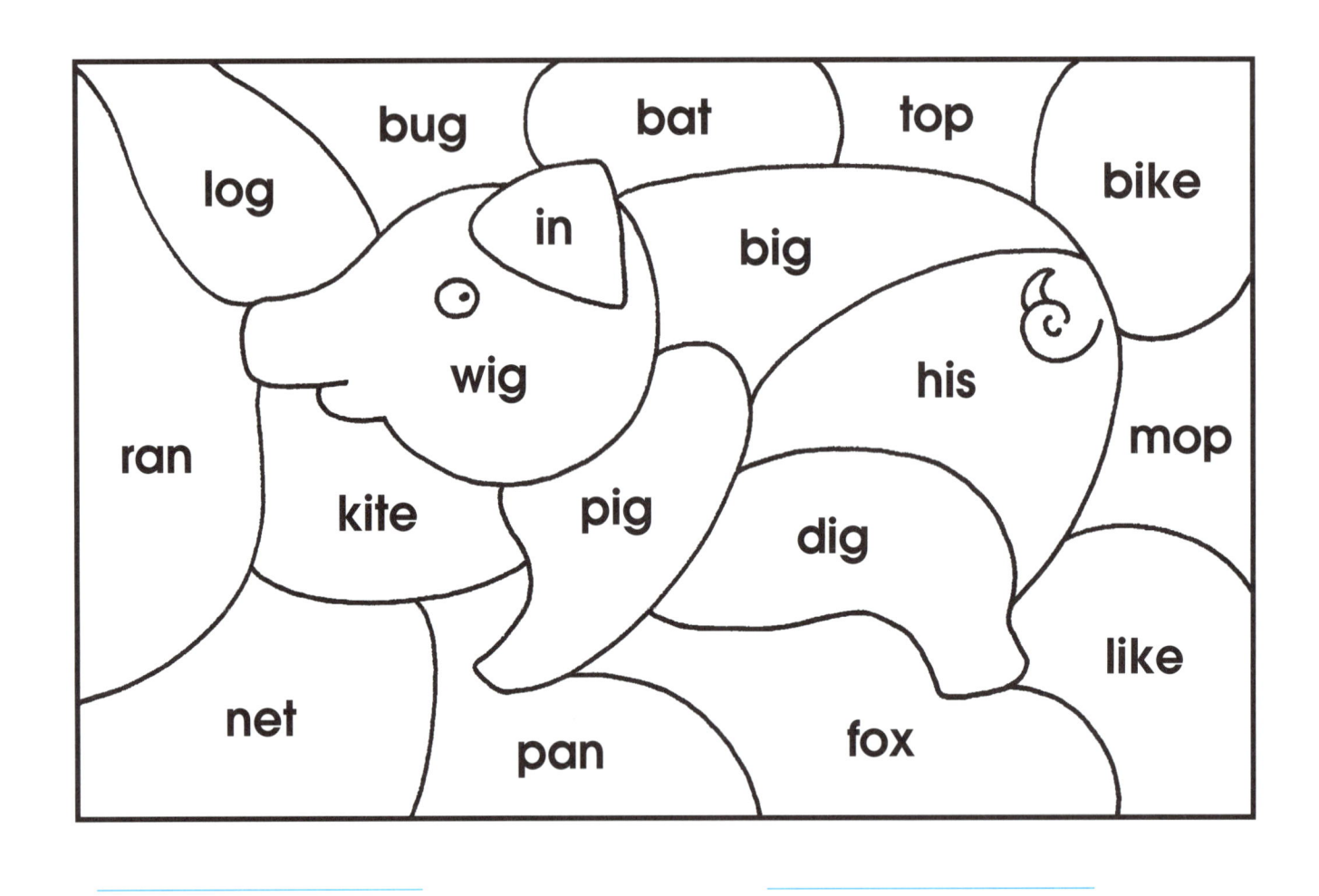

```
log     bug     bat         top
                in                  bike
                    big
        wig             his
ran                                 mop
    kite    pig     dig
                                    like
    net         pan     fox
```

Words with Short o and Short u

Write words from the box to answer the questions.

> fox   sock   box   pot

1. You put me on your foot. What am I? _____

2. I hold toys for you. What am I? _____

3. Mom uses me to cook. What am I? _____

4. I am an animal. What am I? _____

a b c d e f g h i j k l m n o p q r s t u v w x y z
Write the words below in ABC order.

> us   hug   sun

5. _____   6. _____   7. _____

Review

Say the word for each picture.
Write the missing vowel **a**, **e**, **i**, **o**, or **u**.

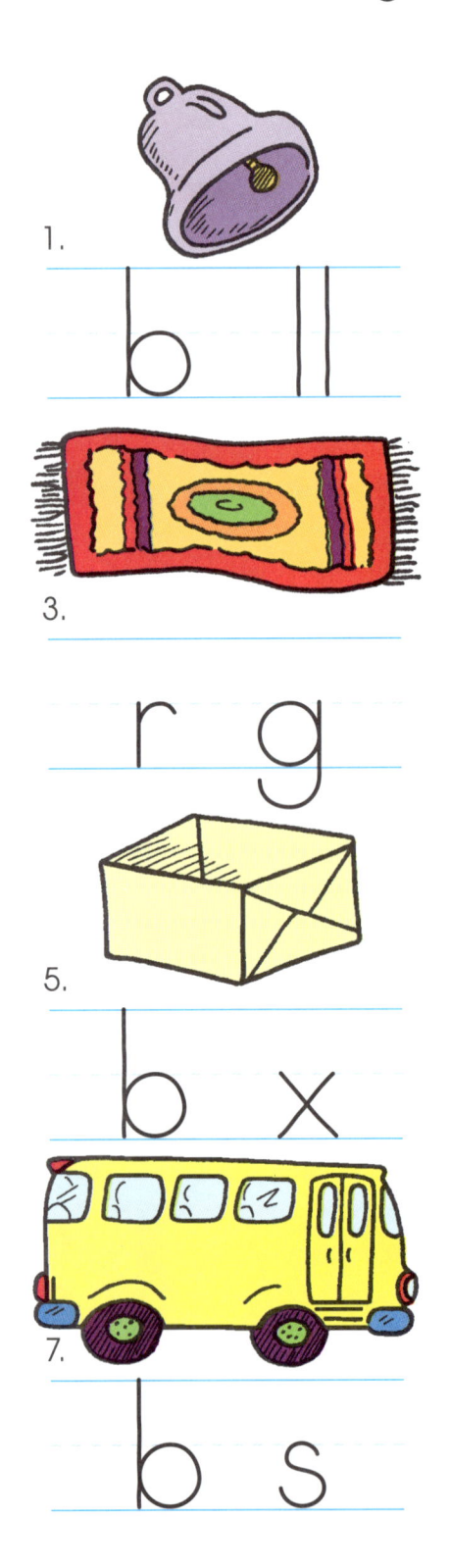

1. b _ ll
2. b _ b
3. r _ g
4. b _ t
5. b _ x
6. v _ n
7. b _ s
8. w _ b

Words with Long a and Long e

Write a **long a** word from the box in each blank.

| game | rake |
| vase | gate |

Bring a _____ to pile the leaves.

We will pick flowers to put in a _____.

Then we can play a _____ of tag.

Don't go past the _____.

Circle the **long e** words.

net　　　tree　　　he　　　seed

see　　　get　　　ten　　　bee

Words with Long i

Write the **long i** words.
Then color the **long i** words in the picture **purple**.

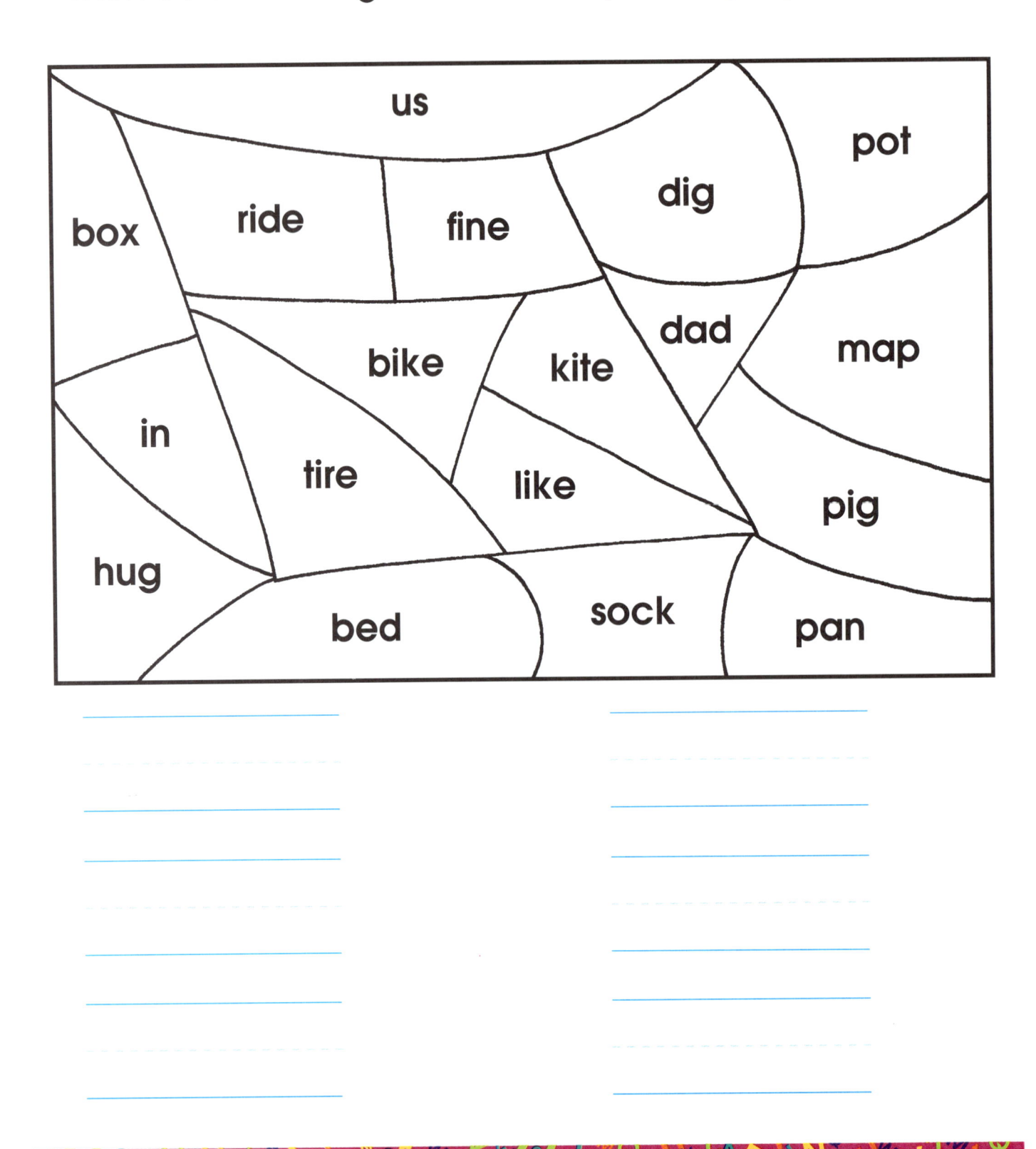

us	
box ride fine	dig pot
	dad map
bike kite	
in tire like	pig
hug bed sock	pan

Words with Long o and Long u

Write words from the box to answer the questions.

> nose   rope   note   home

1. You can tie things with me. What am I?

2. You use me to smell. What am I?

3. You live in me. What am I?

4. You write me. What am I?

a b c d e f g h i j k l m n o p q r s t u v w x y z
Write the words below in ABC order.

> mule   rule   cute

5. _____   6. _____   7. _____

Review

Write five sentences. Use a word from the box in each sentence.

game	home	in
like	Dad	

1.

2.

3.

4.

5.

Answer Key

Page 36
1. fan 2. pie
3. rain 4. cat
5. hat 6. man
7. tie 8. kite

Page 37
1. leaf 2. dog
3. ball 4. queen
5. yarn 6. goat
7. nine 8. soap

Page 38
1. pig 2. sun
3. cup 4. tub
5. nail 6. fox
7. bear 8. drum

Page 39
1. bed 2. seal
3. car 4. elf
5. zero 6. bus
7. cat 8. book

Page 40
1. man 2. mop
3. pen 4. sun
5. bib 6. pan
7. bug 8. ten

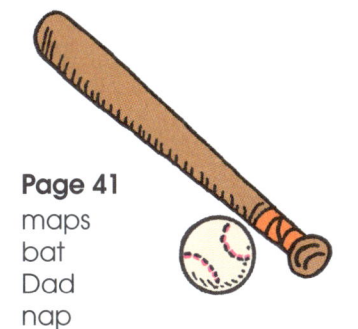

Page 41
maps
bat
Dad
nap
tent, bed, pen, let, net

Page 42
in, his, wig,
big, pig, dig

Page 43
1. sock
2. box
3. pot
4. fox
5. hug
6. sun
7. us

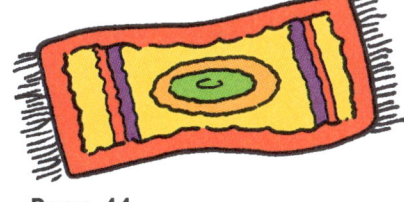

Page 44
1. bell 2. bib
3. rug 4. bat
5. box 6. van
7. bus 8. web

Page 45
rake
vase
game
gate
see, tree, he, seed, bee

Page 46
kite, ride,
fine, tire,
bike, like

Page 47
1. rope
2. nose
3. home
4. note
5. cute
6. mule
7. rule

Page 48
Answers will vary but should include the words *game, home, in, like,* and *Dad.*

©1997 School Zone Publishing Company

49

I Can Read!

◆ **Write a word or number to finish each sentence.**

1. My name is _____ .

2. I am _____ years old.

3. I have _____ brothers.

4. I have _____ sisters.

5. I can _____ this book!

◆ **Read your story. Draw a picture of your family.**

This is me with my family.

At the Park

◆ **Look at the picture of the park. Write how many.**

1. swings

2. seesaws

3. slides

4. benches

◆ **Circle the one that has more.**

5.  swings   or    benches

6.  benches   or    slides

7.  slides   or    seesaws

8.  seesaws   or    swings

A Party!

Come to a Party!

Please come.

who: Jenny
what: Jenny's birthday
where: Jenny's house
what day: May 5
what time: 2:00 PM

◆ **Read the note. Then answer the questions.**

1. Who is having the party?	Jenny	birthday
2. What is the party for?	birthday	house
3. Where will the party be?	Jenny	house
4. What day is the party?	May 5	2:00 PM
5. What time is the party?	May 5	2:00 PM

6. What will you bring to the party?

I will bring _____

Get a Pet!

◆ Read the picture story.

Do you want a dog? Go to   a pet store. Pick out a dog.  Take your dog home. What  will you name your dog?

◆ Show how to buy a pet. Number the pictures 1, 2, 3, and 4 in order.

1. Pick out a pet.

2. Take your pet home.

3. Go to a pet store.

4. Name your pet.

Shoes!

◆ **Draw a line from each sentence to the right shoes.**

1. These are red. A.

2. These have laces. B.

3. Those are purple. C.

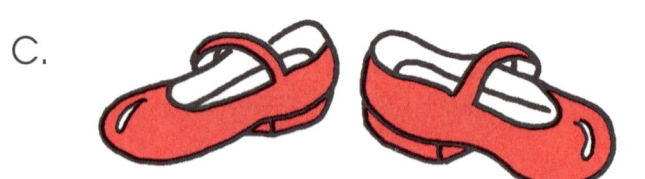

4. Those are for races. D.

5. These are for babies. E.

6. These are for snow. F.

7. These are for clowns. G.

8. Those warm your toes! H.

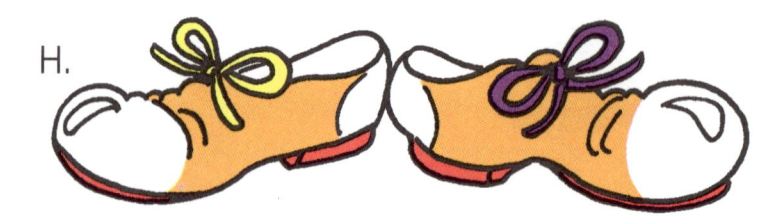

Which One Does Not Belong?

◆ **Circle the one in each group that does not belong.**

1.
2.
3.
4.
5.
6.

Opposites Puzzle

◆ Read the clues.
Write the opposite words in the puzzle.
Use these words if you need help.

cold   down   go   left   lost   out   no

Across ▶

1. found
3. hot
5. in
6. yes

Down ▼

1. right
2. stop
4. up

Find the Message!

◆ **Follow the directions.
Then read the message that is left.**

1. Color the Y boxes **red**.
2. Color the C boxes **blue**.
3. Color the J boxes **orange**.
4. Color the H boxes **brown**.
5. Color the Z boxes **black**.

Y	I	C	J	Z	L	I	K	E	C
R	E	D	C	J	Z	Y	H	J	Y
H	Z	Y	F	L	O	W	E	R	S
A	N	D	Y	P	U	R	P	L	E
C	J	B	A	L	L	O	O	N	S

◆ **Write the message.**

_____

_____

_____ .

Write a Story!

◆ **Draw one more thing that belongs in each group.**

The Beach

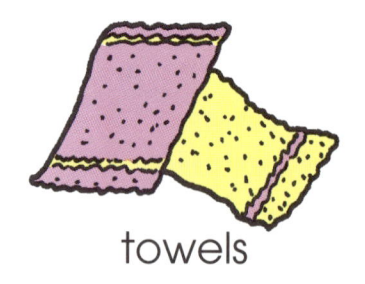

towels   fins   goggles

A Picnic

drinks   dishes   food

◆ **Use one set of words from above to write a riddle. Read your riddle to a friend.**

I am going somewhere. I want to get there. I will take some _____   _____, some _____, and some _____. Can you guess where I'm going? The answer is _____.

58

In My Garden

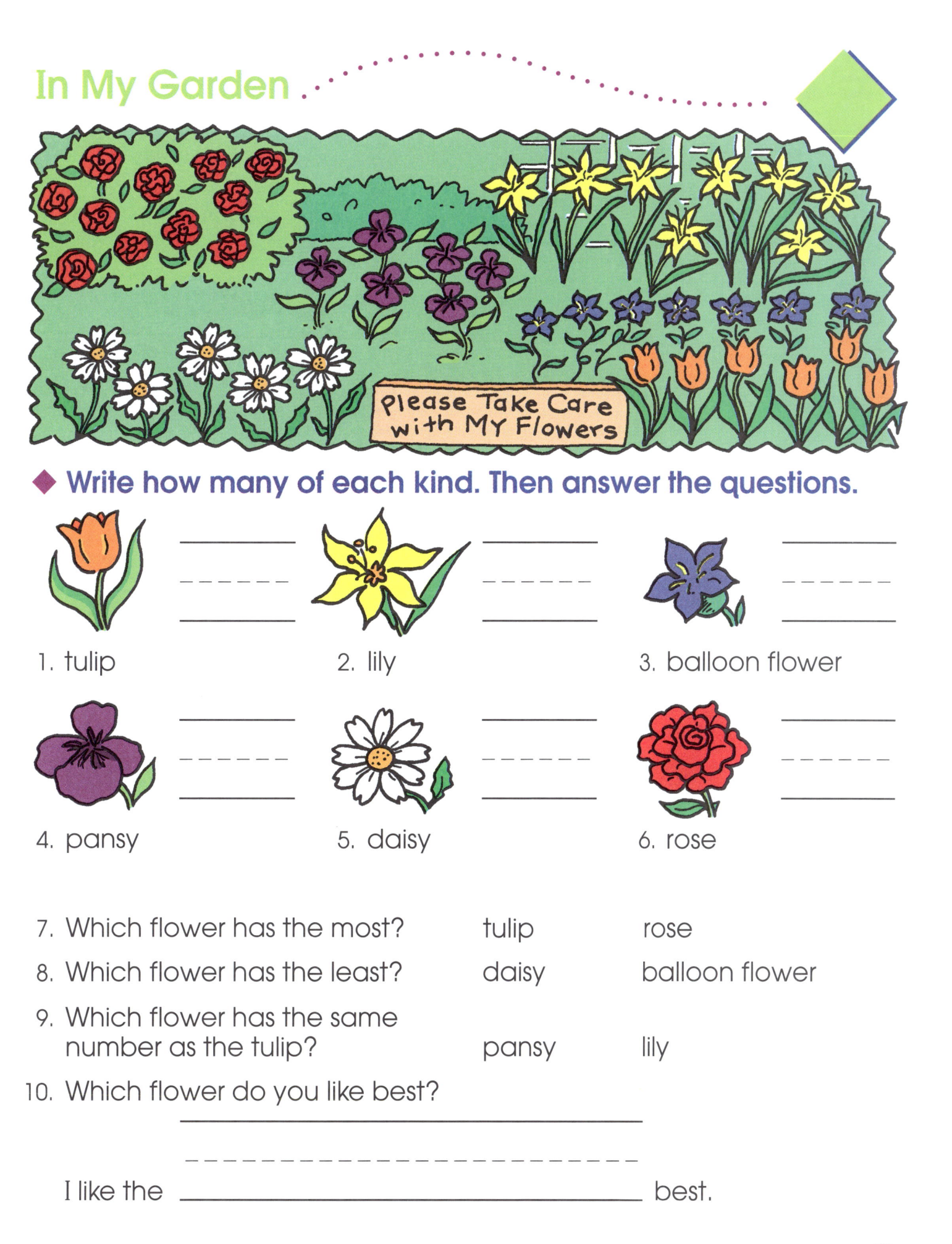

Please Take Care with My Flowers

◆ **Write how many of each kind. Then answer the questions.**

1. tulip _____
2. lily _____
3. balloon flower _____
4. pansy _____
5. daisy _____
6. rose _____

7. Which flower has the most?   tulip   rose
8. Which flower has the least?   daisy   balloon flower
9. Which flower has the same number as the tulip?   pansy   lily
10. Which flower do you like best?

_____

I like the _____ best.

©1997 School Zone Publishing Company

Make a Sandwich!

♦ **Read how to make a sandwich.**

Ham-and-Cheese Sandwich

What you need: **2** slices of bread, some ham, some cheese

1. Get **2** slices of bread.
2. Put some ham on **1** slice.
3. Put some cheese on the ham.
4. Put **1** slice of bread on top.
5. Eat!

♦ **Number the pictures 1, 2, 3, and 4 in order.**

1.

2.

3.

4.

60

Mystery Bus

◆ **Read the picture story.**

Amy got on the bus. It was her first bus ride ever. The driver showed Amy her seat. The bus stopped many times. Other kids got on. Where was the bus going?

◆ **Read the story. Then answer the questions.**

1. What did Amy get on?	bus	boat
2. Who showed Amy where to sit?	mother	driver
3. Who got on when the bus stopped?	dogs	kids
4. Did Amy ride a bus before?	yes	no
5. Did the bus stop a lot?	yes	no

6. Where was the bus going? _____

Hats!

◆ **Draw a line from each sentence to the right hat.**

1. Wear one to cook.

2. Wear this to the game.

3. Wear a helmet to ride.

4. Wear a hat with a name.

5. Wear a hat that is soft.

6. Wear one that is gray.

7. Wear a hat made of straw.

8. Wear a Happy Birthday!

A.

B.

C.

D.

E.

F.

G.

H.

©1997 School Zone Publishing Company

Which Is Real?

◆ **Circle each animal that seems real.**

1.

2.

3.

4.

What Do You Know?

◆ Read the clues.
Write the answers in the puzzle.
Use these words if you need help.

cold   dry   new   open   closed   hot   wet   old

Across ▶

1. No one is in the school.
   The school is ____.

5. I got these shoes long ago.
   These shoes are ____.

6. Mom just bought a car.
   The car is ____.

Down ▼

1. It is snowing outside.
   It is ____.

2. People are shopping.
   The store is ____.

3. I wiped water off the floor.
   Now the floor is ____.

4. Dinner is cooking in the oven.
   The oven is ____.

7. The dog is in the rain.
   The dog is ____.

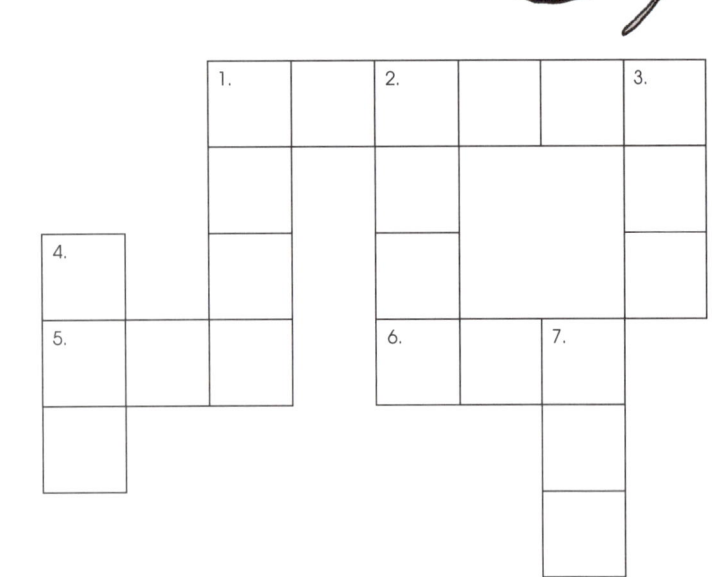

Who's That?

◆ **Read the clues. Then write each name under the right picture.**

Mia always wears red.
Kenji never wears blue.
Sara has a green hat.

Ty has purple shoes.
Mimi likes to paint.
Bob wears the color of the sky.

1. _____

2. _____

3. _____

4. _____

5. _____

6. _____

©1997 School Zone Publishing Company

65

Play Toss the Penny!

◆ **Read about this game. Then answer the questions.**

Want to play a game? Play Toss the Penny! You need 10 pennies and a muffin tin.

Put the tin near a wall. Stand about 10 steps away. Toss a penny. Try to get it in a hole. How many pennies can you get in?

1. Where should you put the muffin tin?

   near a wall

   under a bed

2. Where should you stand?

   5 steps away

   10 steps away

3. What should you do with the penny?

   toss it

   spin it

4. Where do you want the penny to go?

   in your pocket

   in the hole

◆ **Circle how many pennies you need to play this game.**

5.

©1997 School Zone Publishing Company

Silly Man!

I know a silly man,
who walks on his hands.
He has a silly car,
but it doesn't go too far.
And in his silly town,
shops are upside down.
Tell me if you can,
when you see this silly man.

◆ **Read the poem. Circle the answer to each question.**

1. Which one is the silly man?

2. Which car is his?

3. Which hat might be his?

4. Which pet might be his?

©1997 School Zone Publishing Company

What's Next?

◆ **Look at each picture. Then draw what happens next.**

1. It is time to cool off.

2. It is time to play.

3. It is time for lunch.

4. The sun gets hot.

68

©1997 School Zone Publishing Company

Find a Rhyme!

Words that rhyme sound the same at the end.
Pan and **can** rhyme. **Mike** and **bike** rhyme.

◆ **Circle the word in each row that does not rhyme.**

1. dog   log   bird   hog

2. man   pin   fan   can

3. boy   boat   coat   goat

4. two   shoe   blue   bow

©1997 School Zone Publishing Company

69

Get Through the Maze!

♦ **Follow the directions to put the crayons away.**

Use a red line to put the red crayon away.

Use a yellow line to put the yellow crayon away.

Use a blue line to put the blue crayon away.

Use a green line to put the green crayon away.

♦ **Write your answer on the line.**

My favorite color is _____ .

Peanut Butter

I like peanut butter. You can eat it on bread. You can eat it on crackers. You can eat it with jam. I like to eat it on apples.

Peanut butter is made from peanuts and oil. The peanuts are ground up. A bit of oil is added to make peanut butter. It's good for you, too!

◆ **Read the story. Then answer the questions.**

1. What are four ways to eat peanut butter?

   on _____   with _____

   on _____   on _____

2. What is peanut butter made from?

   _____ and _____

3. How do you like to eat peanut butter?

   I like to eat peanut butter _____ .

Break the Code!

Lars saw Sid at school. Sid gave Lars a note.

The note was in code. Lars could not read it. Will you help Lars break the code?

20-15 12-1-18-19,
12-5-20-19 16-12-1-25 19-16-25.
3-15-13-5 20-15 13-25 8-15-21-19-5
1-6-20-5-18 19-3-8-15-15-12.
6-18-15-13 19-9-4

◆ **Write the letter under each number. Then read the message.**

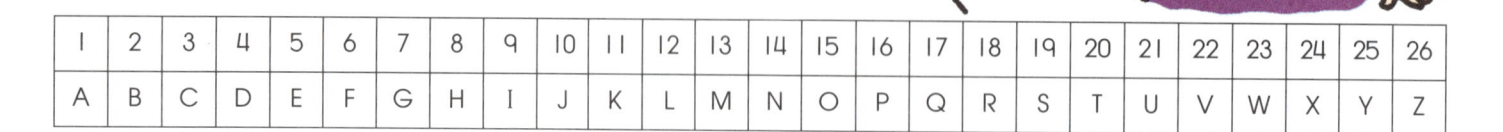

1	2	3	4	5	6	7	8	9	10	11	12	13	14	15	16	17	18	19	20	21	22	23	24	25	26
A	B	C	D	E	F	G	H	I	J	K	L	M	N	O	P	Q	R	S	T	U	V	W	X	Y	Z

20 15   12 1 18 19 ,

12 5 20 19 ,   16 12 1 25   19 16 25 .

3 15 13 5   20 15   13 25   8 15 21 19 5

1 6 20 5 18   19 3 8 15 15 12 .

6 18 15 13 ,   19 9 4

72

Putting Things Away

Do you put things away? That makes them easier to find later.

Lisa puts her toys away when she is done playing. She puts the art things in the art box. She puts toys in the toy box. She puts books in the bookshelf.

◆ **Help Lisa put things away. Draw a line to show where each thing goes.**

©1997 School Zone Publishing Company

At the Circus

◆ **Look at the picture.**
Color the boxes to show how many you see.

ringmaster							
clown							
lion							
dog							
elephant							

©1997 School Zone Publishing Company

Book Covers

Book covers tell the name of a book. They tell who wrote the book. They may tell who drew the pictures, too.

(Book cover shown: MY VALENTINE BOOK, Written by Tyrone James, Pictures by Robert James)

◆ **Read the book cover. Then answer the questions.**

1. Circle the things book covers tell.

   who wrote the book   the name of the book

   when the book was made   who drew the pictures

2. Who wrote this book?

   _____

   _____

3. Who drew the pictures?

   _____

   _____

4. What is this book about?

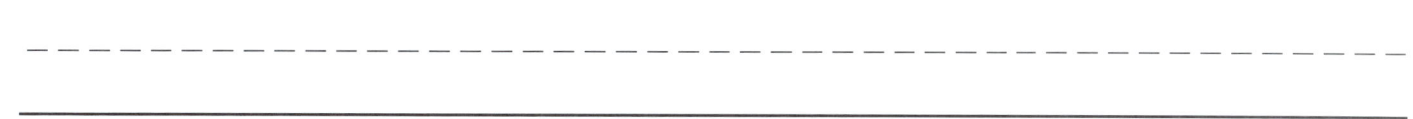

   _____

   _____

Unscramble Puzzle

◆ **Unscramble the clue words.
Write the words in the puzzle.
Use these words if you need help.**

blue   boat   drum   ever   into   mine   tree

Across ▶

1. lube
3. mudr
5. iton
6. veer

Down ▼

1. oatb
2. eret
4. nmie

I Can Read and Write!

◆ **Use one list of words below. Finish the story. Read your story to a friend.**

List A

store   dad   a book   people

List B

circus   mom   a balloon   clowns

Today I will go to the _____ .

My _____ will go with me.

It will be fun! I will buy _____ .

I will see many _____ .

I will say "Hello" to everyone. And I will read every word I see!

Answer Key

Page 50
1. (name)
2. (age)
3. (# of brothers)
4. (# of sisters)
5. Possible answer: read

Page 51
1. 6 swings
3. 2 slides
5. swings
7. seesaws
2. 3 seesaws
4. 3 benches
6. benches
8. swings

Page 52
1. Jenny
2. birthday
3. house
4. May 5
5. 2:00 PM
6. Answers will vary.

Page 53
1. 2
2. 3
3. 1
4. 4

Page 54
1. C
2. B
3. A
4. F
5. D
6. E
7. H
8. G

Page 55
1. wagon
3. ring
5. cake
2. car
4. swimsuit
6. blue jeans

Page 56

	1.l	o	s	t
2.g		e		
3.c	o	l	d	4.f
		5.o	u	t
		w		
		6.n	o	

Page 57
I like red flowers and purple balloons.

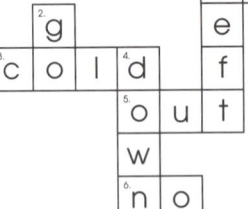

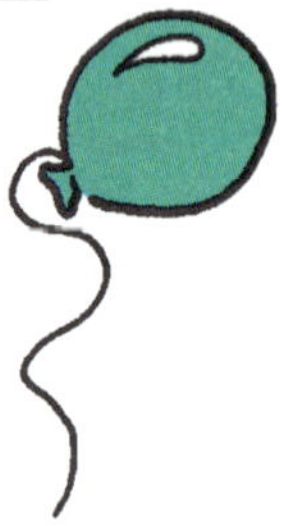

Page 58
Child should add one picture to each group. towels, fin, goggles, to the beach or drinks, dishes, food, on a picnic

Page 59
1. 6
4. 6
7. rose
8. daisy
9. pansy
10. Answers will vary.
2. 8
5. 5
3. 7
6. 11

Page 60
1. 4
2. 1
3. 3
4. 2

Page 61
1. bus
2. driver
3. kids
4. no
5. yes
6. school

Page 62
1. C
2. B
3. A
4. E
5. F
6. D
7. H
8. G

Page 63
1. (left) cat drinking
2. (right) dog jumping
3. (left) macaw on branch
4. (left) shark in water

78 ©1997 School Zone Publishing Company

Answer Key

Page 64

(crossword)
- 1. closed
- 2. open
- 3. dry
- 4. hi
- 5. old
- 6. new
- 7. wet

Page 65
1. Sara
2. Ty
3. Mia
4. Kenji
5. Mimi
6. Bob

Page 66
1. near a wall
2. 10 steps away
3. toss it
4. in the hole
5. 10 pennies

Page 67
1. (right) silly man
2. (left) green car
3. (right) curly hat
4. (left) silly pet

Page 68
Suggested pictures:
1. child swimming
2. child skating
3. child eating
4. snow person melted

Page 69
1. bird
2. pin
3. boy
4. bow

Page 70
Child should use the color of each crayon to draw the line to the box.

Answers will vary.

Page 71
1. bread
   crackers
   jam
   apples
2. peanuts, oil
3. Answers will vary.

Page 72
To Lars,
Let's play spy. Come to my house after school.
From Sid

Page 73
books to bookshelf
toys to toy box
art supplies (paper, paint, brushes) to art box

Page 74
ringmaster (1 box colored)
clown (4 boxes colored)
lion (3 boxes colored)
dog (5 boxes colored)
elephant (3 boxes colored)

Page 75
1. who wrote the book
   the name of the book
   who drew the pictures
2. Tyrone James
3. Robert James
4. valentines

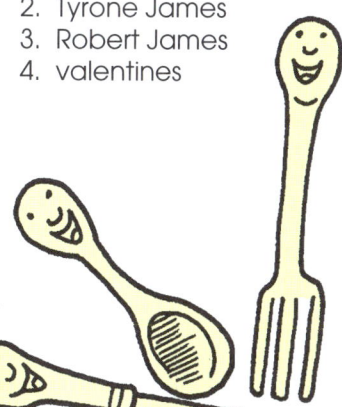

Page 76

(crossword)
- 1. blue
- 2. t
- 3. drum
- 4. m
- 5. into
- 6. ever
- boat
- teen

Page 77
Words used should be *store, dad, a book, people* or *circus, mom, a balloon, clowns.*

©1997 School Zone Publishing Company

79

CD-ROM Navigational Chart

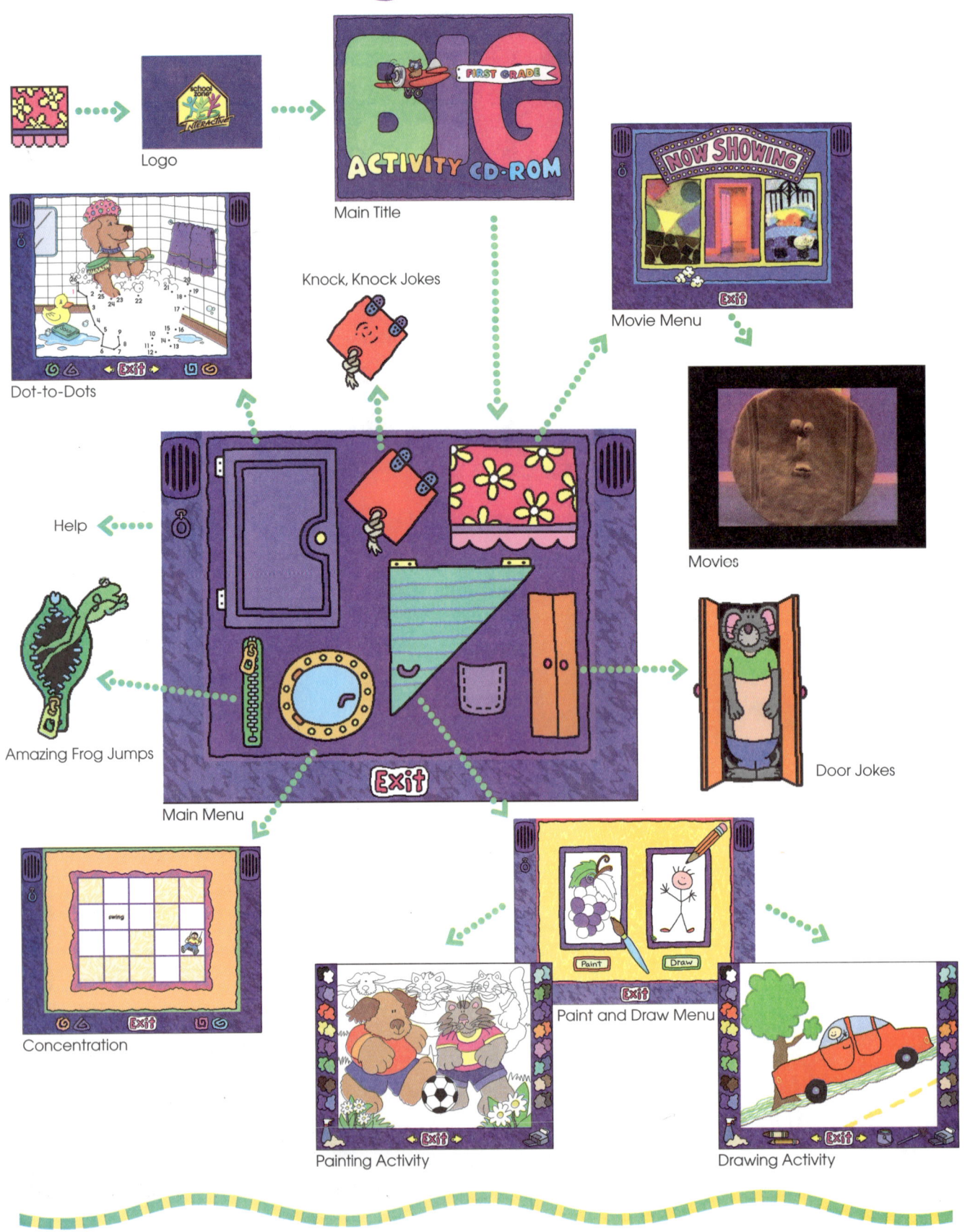

Logo

Main Title

Knock, Knock Jokes

Movie Menu

Dot-to-Dots

Help

Movies

Amazing Frog Jumps

Main Menu

Door Jokes

Concentration

Paint and Draw Menu

Painting Activity

Drawing Activity

80

©1997 School Zone Publishing Company
First Grade CD-ROM and Workbook 08210